PORTFOLIO I

METROPOLITAN SEMINARS IN ART

Great Periods in Painting

PORTFOLIO I

The Quick and the Dead: REALISM VS. THE SALON

BY JOHN CANADAY

ART EDITOR AND CRITIC
THE NEW YORK TIMES

THE METROPOLITAN MUSEUM OF ART

THE QUICK AND THE DEAD

Realism vs. the Salon

IN THE nineteenth century France was the country in which painting flourished most vigorously. The names of the painters who changed the course of art and set the pace for the rest of the world are French names— Courbet, Manet, Monet, Renoir, Degas, Cézanne, Gauguin, and Seurat among them— or the names of foreigners, like the Dutchman Van Gogh, who made France their adopted home because it offered them the kind of spiritual and intellectual nourishment they needed. Yet in varying degrees these men were ignored or attacked by the critics and derided by the public. Those among them without private means suffered great hardship, were sometimes without money for food and paints, before they fought their way to recognition— if they were fortunate enough to achieve recognition before the end of their lives. During the second half of the century, France seemed to be trying systematically to stifle the creative genius of artists who are now recognized as great, while mediocre painters became rich and famous.

In retrospect the situation seems unforgiveable, but it is explainable. The men responsible for such a contradictory state of affairs were sincere in their belief that they were defending great traditions against the assaults of madmen, charlatans, and incompetents. Just why they thought so may be more clear if we look at the Salon of 1855 and some of the events connected with it.

In 1855 France held the greatest yet in the series of world fairs that fascinated a Europe watching itself being transformed from decade to decade by new machines, new means of communication, new discoveries in science, new everything. Four years previously, England had staged The Great Exhibition of the Works of Industry of All Nations, 1851, an immensely successful affair held in the Crystal Palace. France now set about the job of surpassing it with the Exposition Universelle. Among the attractions was to be the largest exhibition of fine art ever held anywhere.

Every foreign artist of any consequence (and many of no consequence, as we see them now) was invited to represent his country. France was determined to demonstrate her preeminence in the arts by enlarging the annual Salon to display current work along with retrospective shows of the most important men. Ingres, who was a venerable seventy-five and the lofty deity of the Academy, was represented by forty pictures in a separate gallery. Delacroix, who at fifty-seven had fought through to academic recognition without ceasing to stand out against academic pedantry, was similarly honored. There were other major figures who are hardly familiar names today, such as Alexandre Gabriel Decamps (1803–1860), whose romantic oriental scenes were preferred to those of Delacroix by the majority of his contemporaries. The total number of pictures exhibited was around five thousand. Into what limbo have so many of these now "forgotten favorites" disappeared?

Romanticism by this time was neither a scandal nor a revolution. The die-hard classicists and their younger followers remained the conservative core of the Academy, but the romantics were accepted as the "modern" element in official circles. The forces of conservatism had recently become concentrated against an upstart from the provinces named Gustave Courbet (1819–1877), the son of a prosperous farmer, who had dared to challenge both factions by rejecting idealism in either direction. Courbet's "Show me an angel and I will paint one" was his way of saying that he rejected not only angels but also the gods of classical legend and the romantic heroes of medieval times and exotic places. He dedicated himself to painting the world around him, a world immediately visible and tangible and commonplace. He found French peasants a fitter subject than ancient Romans or Arab chieftains. The outcroppings of rock in the countryside around his native Ornans were more exciting to him than the Acropolis with its temples or the orient with its seraglios. He went out of his way to offend conservative painters and a conservative public by such unidealistic statements as his famous bit of advice to young painters, that it was better to paint dunghills than not to paint from nature at all.

Courbet was a particularly galling thorn to the academicians because a fluke had made him invulnerable to their strongest weapon, rejection from the annual Salon. Inclusion or rejection could make or break a career; if a painter's work was not accepted for Salon exhibition he had a difficult time exhibiting it anywhere else. Private dealers were not as numerous as they are today. There were almost none adventurous enough to take on a painter without the official accolade of Salon exhibition. The Salon juries had virtual control of professional life or death over unknown or rising artists, and they frequently abused their function through favoritism and spite.

But Courbet was beyond their reach. In 1849 the Salon had gone through one of its several short-lived periods of reform. The revolution of the year before had resulted in a no-jury Salon. Still chastened, the jury of 1849 was an exceptionally liberal one. Courbet, not yet well known, was awarded a medal for his *After Dinner at Ornans*, a somewhat romantically observed picture of simple people gathered around a table and an excellent piece of painting by any standard. After receiving a medal, a painter had the privilege of exhibiting *hors concours* in future Salons—that is, without passing the jury. Courbet took advantage of this privilege to exhibit nine pictures the following year and became a storm center with the painting called *A Burial at Ornans* (*Figure 1*).

A Burial at Ornans shows a group of peasants and middle-class provincials around an open grave. It is beautifully painted, with Courbet's typical rich, oily surface. Certainly the effect today is that of a picture at least as reverent and dignified as it is realistic in its presentation of common people. In the rich shadows and mellow lights we must even feel a romantic quality. But in contrast with the idealism of the best Salon painting and the sentimentalism of the run of the mill, the subject and its treatment seemed crude and vulgar. In the same Salon Courbet exhibited his *Stonebreakers*, showing a peasant man and a boy at this hard labor. Both pictures, and their painter, were called "socialistic."

Until now Courbet had held no political views, but he liked the socialist label and thereafter he flaunted it. He was a rather rough and simple man, far from being intellectual, and his "socialism" was never well assimilated either into his thinking or his life, or into his painting for that matter. He formed a friendship with the socialist philosopher Pierre Joseph Proudhon, and called himself "not only socialist, but furthermore democratic and republican, in a word a partisan of all revolution and above all a realist, a sincere friend of the true truth" (a statement that shows just about

Figure 1

how clear his political thinking was). The great liberal Zola summed it up pretty well when he said that the "poor, dear master" had a bad case of "democratic indigestion."

But Courbet enjoyed the fracas stirred up by his pseudosocialist pronouncements, especially since as a well-to-do man he did not have to worry about sales. When he did sell, to perceptive collectors, he sold for good prices. In the meantime he continued to exhibit in the Salon as he chose to, to the impotent fury of the reactionary academicians.

The Pavilion of Realism

But to return to the Salon of 1855; that year's jury had its chance to strike back. Because of the unusual nature of the Salon as a part of the Exposition Universelle, the *hors concours* privilege for medalists was suspended. Courbet had been planning to deliver a manifesto of realism, in competition with the Ingres and Delacroix exhibitions, by entering a group of pictures that included *A Burial at Ornans* once more and, above all, a huge picture that was to be his *Oath of the Horatii*, his *Raft of the Medusa*, his *Massacres of Scio*—a picture with the naïvely egocentric title, *The Painter's Studio: A Real Allegory Summarizing a Seven-Year Phase of My Artistic Life* (*Figure 2*). The jury, no doubt some with glee, rejected both pictures.

Undaunted, Courbet decided to hold his own one-man exhibition by building a structure to house it, called the Pavilion of Realism. But he did not have the success that David had had when he exhibited *The Sabines* for a fee or that Géricault had had when he put *The Raft of the Medusa* on the road. Hardly anyone came. Courbet did not even recoup the expense of the Pavilion. But he might have been comforted if he could have read a few sentences written by another painter, one who had the habit of jotting down his activities and thoughts in diary form. "I went to see Courbet's exhibition," wrote Delacroix in his now famous journal. "There alone for nearly an hour. I discovered a masterpiece in his rejected picture. I couldn't tear myself away from it. They have refused, there, one of the most extraordinary works of our time."

As a manifesto of realism, *The Painter's Studio* is confused and inconsistent. It is in the first place a synthetic conglomeration of allegorical figures, not in line with the theories of realism even though the allegory is expressed in figures of ordinary folk. To the left are gathered types, mostly rustic, that Courbet

7

Figure 2

often painted. The muzzy symbolism includes a death's head lying on a copy of the periodical *Le Journal des Débats*, perhaps a comment on censorship or on the low state of critical journalism; an artist's manikin suspended on a stake may be a symbol of academic art; a second-hand dealer (Commerce?), a buffoon (the Theater with its illusions?), a priest, and a prostitute, these latter being in Courbet's mind representatives of elements that preyed on the people.

On the right are friends and patrons representing the arts. Baudelaire, reading a book, represents the Art of Poetry, Proudhon is there to represent Social Philosophy, and other identifiable figures represent Prose, Realistic Poetry, and Music. The man and woman in the right foreground represent knowledgeable art lovers in general.

There are many beautiful and a few hurried passages of painting in these groups, but in the center foreground, where Courbet paints at an easel while a nude model and a small boy look on admiringly, the painting is magnificent. Here the artist is at his best in spite

of the contradictory artificiality of the arrangement. If there is any symbolism in the nude and the child, it must be guessed at; but such ideas may be dismissed as not pertinent to Courbet's art, since the central group is indeed Courbet's manifesto in a more important way. Here he demonstrates what he was, purely and simply and superbly a painter, so enraptured with the world that he could conceive of nothing more joyously satisfying than to reflect it in images recalling its wonderful reality and its substance.

Realism for Courbet was not the reproduction of small details microscopically recorded. The breadth, the mass, the solidity, the palpability of objects stirred him beyond anything else. His *Two Girls on the Banks of the Seine* (Plate I 1) takes us into the world he loved and painted with a full, unanalytical sensuousness that could seem coarse (as it did to so many of his contemporaries) if its opulence did not represent such a fine example of pure painting. The paint that makes up the images of great masses of cloth, laces, and ribbons, of firm, weighty flesh, of cool earth and grass, is a sensuous experience in itself. With it the artist captures and glorifies his response to the good things of physical life.

Two Girls on the Banks of the Seine can be compared with Giorgione's *The Concert* (Plate E4), in which sensuous experience is equally intense, but idealized. The contrast between the pictures, to the disadvantage of neither, is the essence of Courbet's objection to painting angels. He was a man of the nineteenth century, an age that had dismissed the ideal aesthetic in its daily experience. It was the age of the common man triumphant. The triumph brought with it some appalling vulgarities, a crassness and commonplaceness that was aesthetically indefensible. But as an artist who summarized common experience at its highest level Courbet glorified this experience without attempting to ennoble or purify it. Since he was not a sixteenth-century Venetian, he painted two girls lying in the shade on an ordinary riverbank instead of two idealized nudes accompanied by satin-clad musicians in an idyllic landscape.

We might compare *Two Girls on the Banks of the Seine* with another picture we have discussed, Rubens' *Rape of the Daughters of Leucippus* (Plate F5), remembering that Rubens was a princely painter in a princely age. Courbet as much as Rubens loved the moist richness of flesh, the sheen of cascading hair, the textures of stuffs. Granting the difference between the baroque splendor of Rubens' century and the bourgeois common sense of Courbet's, the two pictures are not dissimilar in their proclamation of the glory of sentience.

As a personality Courbet was not the most engaging man in Paris, and no doubt his arrogance accounted for some of the attacks that now seem so exaggerated when we look at his paintings. Before he became grossly fat in middle age, he was an unusually handsome man, and he has left a series of self-portraits to tell us so. An early one called *The Man with the Leather Belt* was in the Salon of 1849, the year Courbet won his medal. This is a highly romanticized picture, which suggests why Courbet's threat as a potential realist was not apparent to the jury at that time. Five years later he painted as extraordinary a self-portrait, certainly, as could be found anywhere, the picture always called *Bonjour, Monsieur Courbet* (Plate I2), a title with mocking overtones, although Courbet called it *The Encounter*. The artist shows himself arriving at Montpellier to pay a visit on a patron, the distinguished collector Alfred Bruyas, who has come out with manservant and dog to greet him. Courbet appears at an advantageous angle; his striking profile and his fine figure are played up like those of an actor, while Bruyas and his servant doff their hats in the presence of genius. Yet this self-glorification is so unquestioning that there is a kind of engaging innocence about it.

Courbet was always generous of his time with young painters when they asked him for advice. Parisian cafés had become gathering spots for intellectual and artistic factions, as they still are. Courbet set himself up at one called the Brasserie des Martyrs where his table was surrounded by students, including some who were to be the great men of the impressionist movement. Even more strenuously than Courbet they were to carry on the continuing battle against Salon standards.

The Salon Painters

The Salon gave a large number of awards annually, ranging from a handful of Grand Medals of Honor down through Medals First, Second, and Third Class, and then the usual sop of honorable mentions. The 1855 Salon that rejected Courbet gave Grand Medals of Honor to Delacroix and Ingres, as might be expected, but the sensation of the year was another Grand Medalist named Jean Louis Ernest Meissonier (1815–1891), who had been winning lesser medals since he was twenty-five, who now reached high distinction at forty, and who thereafter won so many honors that new

Figure 3

ones had to be invented for him. He was the first painter in history to receive the Grand Cross of the Legion of Honor. His name today is synonymous with all that is routine and unimaginative in nineteenth-century art.

The emperor selected Meissonier's *La Rixe* (The Brawl), a picture showing some musketeers squabbling in a tavern, as his official gift to Queen Victoria upon the occasion of her visit to the Exposition. Meissonier painted innumerable pictures of this type, literal renditions of costumed models that amused the Salon public and attracted purchasers.

In his later career Meissonier concentrated on incidents from Napoleonic history. The best known of these is *1814: The Campaign in France* (*Figure 3*), showing the dejected leader during the days of defeat. Instead of one costumed model, Meissonier here paints a hundred or so and combines them with great competence in a snowy landscape. There can be absolutely no objection to work of this kind when it is offered for what it is, a kind of

mechanical illustration at an irreproachable technical level in which some of the importance of the event rubs off onto the picture itself. The objection to Meissonier and other Salon painters like him is that they were mistaken for great creative artists when essentially they were stunt men with a superlative knack for mimicry, and—most important—that they were blind to all else in the way of art.

The reason for their popularity is easy to find. The small and cultivated class of patrons that had died with the eighteenth century had been replaced with a new kind, the not very cultivated bourgeois who for a long time has summed up his limitations with a certain pride in the worn boast that he does not know much about art but knows what he likes. What he liked best was a picture telling a little story, preferably one corroborating his hope that he was a fine moral and intellectual specimen. His patronage created the "Salon painter," usually a man who had gone through the academic mill obediently and had emerged with no fur-

10

ther ambition than to find a formula for salable pictures and to repeat it as often as possible.

The archetype of the Salon painter is Jean Léon Gérôme (1824–1904), who won a Medal Second Class in 1855 when he was thirty-one, and thereafter rose steadily year after year, selling as fast as he could paint. His *Pygmalion and Galatea* (Plate 13), which tells the story of a sculptor who fell in love with a statue he had carved and whose prayers were answered by Venus when she brought the statue to life, offers just about everything that the Salon purchaser asked. The technique is slickly impressive (the technical level of Salon painting was very high, and Gérôme was undeniably a superb craftsman); the story is enjoyable for itself but also carries a cultural guarantee, since it is a classical one; the treatment is just erotic enough to please bourgeois taste but not erotic enough to create unease. The special feature of *Pygmalion and Galatea* that reveals more than anything else the nature of Salon taste is the way the statue, still half stone and already half a living woman, changes from white to pink from feet to head. The effect is at best tricky, and today is somehow a bit ludicrous (what we would call "corny," a word applicable to much Salon art), but it supplied the novelty value that made one Salon picture stand out from the competing hundreds around it in the gigantic salesroom that the Salon had become.

Of course it is easy to poke fun at Salon painting, and much of it deserves no better treatment. But imbedded in the mediocre mass there are examples that are too easily dismissed by critics conditioned to the idea that all Salon painting is bad as such. We have seen an exception in a previous discussion, Gérôme's *Duel after the Masquerade* (Portfolio 2, Plate 21). The picture might be looked at again, and the comments reviewed by the reader. We have also seen Cot's *The Storm* (Portfolio 1, Plate 11), which we accompanied with some speculations on Salon painting and the possibility of its eventual return to popularity. Museums are beginning to bring a few Salon pictures up from storage. Sometimes this is because the pictures look not quite so bad as we have been led to believe. More often it is because they are needed to complete a historical summary. A museum has a double function: it may set itself up as an arbiter of taste, but it also tries to provide a visual record of the history of art. Courbet's realism and the further revolt of the impressionists, which we have yet to see, take on additional meanings when we see them against the background of the Salon painting with which they had to compete.

The Paris Salon was by far the most influential arbiter of taste in the nineteenth century, but it had its counterparts in most of the other countries of Europe, and even in America. European sophistications, involving deteriorated echoes of the great traditions (in Gérôme's case, the classical tradition) were less popular on this side of the water than in their homeland. Ambitious collectors imported Salon painting from Europe, but the American equivalent of the European Salon painter was more likely to concentrate on more homely fare. Moral preachments with a strong sentimental flavor were very popular, while nudes were looked at askance by the general public. Most Americans preferred pictures like *Breaking Home Ties* (Plate 14) by Thomas Hovenden (1840–1895). This American of Irish birth studied in America and then in Paris with Cabanel (of whom more later), an academician in Gérôme's general category, and specialized in storytelling pictures with a strong folksy flavor. *Breaking Home Ties* was the most famous of these and the best loved. Even today it attracts a sympathetic audience when it is on exhibition, but during the latter decades of the nineteenth century people used to stand in line to see it. There are still Philadelphians alive who remember that when *Breaking Home Ties* was put on exhibition in a local department store, susceptible lady spectators would yield to tears in front of it.

Only the simplest souls could be so moved

11

today, yet only the most shortsighted critics would deny the picture its considerable virtues. It may be sentimental, but it is an agreeably unpretentious picture, honestly drawn and solidly painted, admirable in the tonality of its warm darks and gentle lights. Recently the museum that owns it lent it to a collector as a substitute for a Picasso of the same size (it is a large picture) that had been borrowed for exhibition. Surrounded by other works in the private collection by such painters as Miró, Mondrian, Klee, and Le Douanier Rousseau, *Breaking Home Ties* held its own better than anyone expected, like a simple but honest country cousin at a fashionable dinner party.

The picture's insuperable defect is that it is not first a painting, not first a work of pictorial art. It is first an anecdote, an illustration, a picture *of* something rather than a creation in its own right. It does not enlarge or clarify our ideas, either intellectual or emotional. It merely stirs up an established set of associations, and rather trite ones at that. It has, in short, all the limitations of Salon painting, although it is refreshingly devoid of the pretensions that made the Salon a vicious force.

The Salon des Refusés

The Salon of 1855 was not a bad one in spite of the unkind things we have been saying here about nineteenth-century Salons in general. The effort to give an honest survey of French painting at its best was apparently sincere, and we must remember that although *A Funeral at Ornans* and *The Painter's Studio* were rejected, the jury did pass some other pictures that Courbet submitted.

But in the following years the juries grew more and more narrow, until finally in 1863 the situation became intolerable. That year the jury accepted or rejected pictures so obviously on the basis of favoritism and spite that objections poured in to the government from every side. The emperor called his Minister of Fine Arts, a snob and a philistine, the Count of Nieuwerkerke, and commanded him to arrange for a second Salon composed of the rejected pictures, to be set up near the regular one. This, the Salon des Refusés, would give the public an opportunity to judge for itself whether the complaints were justified. Painters who did not want their work exhibited under these circumstances were given the privilege of withdrawing it, but the great majority decided to show, even at the risk of future unpleasantness with the Salon proper.

The Salon des Refusés is a landmark in the history of modern art. It was the first public intimation that the juries might not be infallible, and this intimation came from an official source. In effect, the Salon des Refusés proclaimed the artist's right to show his work to the public without subjection to the intermediary judgment of men who might or might not be sympathetic to him. The artist had made the first step towards what, for him, corresponded to freedom of speech.

It would be a pleasure to be able to record that the public, given the chance to see through its own eyes, responded perceptively, but unhappily this was not so. People thronged to the Salon des Refuses, but they came prepared in advance to laugh at the pictures that had been singled out as the academy's victims. The excitement focused on one by Édouard Manet (1832–1883) called *Le Déjeuner sur l'herbe* (*Figure 4*), or *The Picnic*.

Manet, who at this time was thirty-one years old, had combined a rebellious, investigative spirit as a student and novice painter with an extreme personal reserve amounting to haughtiness. Neither of these traits was conducive to popularity with the kind of academician a young painter should set out to please. Yet Manet had made a promising start with *The Guitarist* (*Figure 5*) in the Salon of 1861. He received an honorable mention, which was at least a beginning, and the picture was such a popular success that it was moved to a better position during the exhibition.

But just before the 1863 Salon Manet made

a tactical error with a one-man show at a commercial gallery, Martinet's. The pictures were abusively attacked by conservative critics who had liked *The Guitarist*.

Manet had strengthened his colors considerably, applying theories we will discuss shortly, but the difference between these paintings and the successful *Guitarist* hardly seems great enough to warrant the critical about face. One wonders whether personal antagonisms or professional jealousies were not at work behind the scenes. If not then, they certainly were from then on. The academy and the conservative critics hounded Manet until the last years of his life; and Manet, temperamentally different from Courbet, suffered from these attacks as Courbet never had. He did not enjoy the fracas. He wanted Salon recognition and

official honors; but he wanted first of all to solve certain problems in painting, and in solving them he was unwilling to compromise with conventional standards for an instant, not even for the kind of acclaim he so desired.

The problems Manet set himself had to do with the nature of vision, the technique of a form of realism that would present images of things with the maximum impact, almost the shock, of first sight. His *Torero Saluting* (Plate 15) and the *Woman with a Parrot* (Detail, Plate 16; full picture, *Figure 6*) will show the solution he found. They do not look revolutionary to us, since Manet's innovations have become familiar. Even so, we may recognize the breadth of the color areas in *Torero Saluting* and the economy of formal description in the woman's head as remarkable. In

Figure 4

13

Figure 5

both examples Manet departed from the traditional recipes for color and modeling. In a traditional painting, the colors that blaze in the costume of the torero would have been less intense because they would have been modified by half tones and high lights. Or, to begin with a passage we can see at closer range, the blue ribbon in the woman's hair: in traditional technique the blue would have been composed of a series of gradations changing from a dulled tone in the shadow through a somewhat less dulled one, or half tone, as the ribbon passed into the light. Briefly the "local color," that is, the color of the ribbon itself at its purest intensity, would have appeared. Then it would have paled out in lighter passages and finally would have appeared bleached in the high light. In five shades of blue or bluish color, the pure local color would have appeared in only one passage.

Now, such passages from tone to tone can be beautiful, but to Manet's way of thinking they lacked the force and immediacy of color as we see it. The color we see is reflected light, and its intensity is reduced when in a painting its tonalities are approximated in pigment. To make up for the difference, Manet eliminated the usual grayed half tones and bleached lights common in the work of other painters. The ribbon is painted, essentially, in two bright blues or, rather, two shades of the same blue unadulterated by neutralizing color changes. The vividness of these blues is increased by contrast with the few essential darks, which are reduced to intense concentrations, hardly more than lines, almost black. In minute areas, they emphasize the brilliance of the large color areas rather than spreading into and thus graying them.

The russet hair is similarly treated. An "accurate" rendering would have shown a multitude of changing lights and varying reflected colors. And in the modeling of the features, half tones have been lightened or entirely eliminated, leaving the forms described by a few boldly stroked-in darks in an area of almost flat color. The fingers are described by shadows that have been reduced to thick lines—Manet's famous "black line" which, since it "does not exist in nature," was attacked as heresy.

There is hardly an element here that had not been anticipated, to a lesser degree, by other painters. Goya had said that he wanted to train his brush not to see more than his eye did and had worked in the direction of economical definition. Hals had worked in broad planes. There are similarities between Manet and Zurbarán. Manet's innovations are based on the art of painters who were accepted as fathers of the Salon tradition, which included all the recognized old masters. But instead of plagiarizing the old masters as traditional painters were doing, Manet used their theories as points of departure to develop his own. And he achieved his end: he presents us with images carrying the impact of momen-

Figure 6

tary revelation. Before Manet objects had been described as they are perceived upon continued examination. But an image by Manet has the vivid reality of instant vision, transfixed forever but wonderfully alive.

In such images, the effectiveness depends upon the selection of the few elements that are represented. Manet's problem was to know just which half tones and shadows could be eliminated, to exactly what degree he could simplify the image without weakening it. His problem was the problem of all painters, to create a harmony of parts that would be a consistent whole. Some painters, for instance Jan van Eyck in the Arnolfini portrait (Portfolio 1, Plate 10), created their harmony from a multitude of almost microscopic details. Others, like Velazquez (*The Maids of Honor*, Portfolio 2, Plate 19), created it by careful adjustment of the parts to the proportionate degrees of visibility from a certain distance. Others, like Courbet, created it by making tangible the forms of nature in the essence of their physical mass. But all these painters created images that we must recognize as the result of careful, practiced, and systematic observation of their models in nature. Manet's objective was to work out a way of painting that looked absolutely spontaneous. The wonder of a fine Manet is that it eternalizes an instantaneous effect and does so in a way so expert that we feel that his paintings, the results of study and analysis, are the improvisations of a moment.

The academicians failed to see the calculation behind Manet's effects of spontaneity. They called his painting sloppy and coarse. The exhibition at Martinet's included numerous Spanish subjects similar to the *Torero Saluting*, in which the bright dyes of satins in contrast with dead or glistening blacks gave Manet the opportunity to apply his colors with maximum dramatic effect. Accustomed to the tactful harmonies of Salon painting, the critics compared Manet to Goya, but to Goya "gone mad on the pampas," and his intense

and singing harmonies were called a wild confusion of raw pigment.

Thus, two months after the show at Martinet's, the Salon jury was ready to reject whatever Manet submitted, and he made things easy for them with *The Picnic* which is still a startling picture as it approaches its hundredth birthday. In the seated nude, he pushed his theory to its limits; the figure is a light silhouette of almost flat tone suddenly brought into relief by a few essential concentrated darks. The extraordinary impression of reality thus created makes the presence of the casual, fully clothed young men at the young woman's side even more contradictory, and there is a curious disparity between the three foreground figures and the landscape, with its fourth figure, behind them. The landscape was painted from nature, and the figures in the studio. The combination is not altogether convincing. But as pure painting, *The Picnic* is Manet at top form, centering around the superb nude and the still life of discarded clothing and picnic paraphernalia.

The reader may already have connected the picture with Giorgione's *The Concert*. When *The Picnic* was attacked as immoral, Manet's defenders pointed out that it was only a modern version of this accepted masterpiece. The attackers rejoined, with some justification, that the idealization of the old master and the realism of the Manet invalidated the comparison. Crowds at the Salon des Refusés gathered around *The Picnic* to ridicule it or to enjoy sensations of moral outrage. Manet suffered intensely, but he did not change the direction of his experiments, which were even then on the point of culmination in his undisputed masterpiece, *Olympia* (Plate 17).

Olympia

Olympia is the key picture of mid-nineteenth-century realism. More than any picture of Courbet's it exemplifies the objectivity to which, theoretically, the half-romantic Cour-

Figure 7

bet was dedicated. A young courtesan, unabashedly naked, regards us with a noncommittal gaze. Her rather hard, thick, and short-legged figure is that of a woman of the people, but she is projected neither as a social symbol nor as an ideal. She is an object, an object painted neither more nor less interpretatively than the sheets or the embroidered shawl or the bouquet offered her by a maidservant.

As the complete demonstration of Manet's technique, the figure and the other objects in *Olympia* are revealed to us as if by a flash of light. Manet is now in full control of his method. *The Picnic* tends to break up into the component parts of an assembled picture, but *Olympia* is consistently unified as a single momentary revelation of visual fact.

Manet painted *Olympia* in 1863, the year of the Salon des Refusés, but it was not exhibited until 1865—in that year's Salon. The emperor's displeasure and the increasing number of liberal critics who defended Manet had produced another interval of Salon reform. *Olympia* was accepted and hung, but was then attacked with utmost ferocity. The attacks were more violent than those on *The Picnic*; the picture was compared to "high" game, and the curiosity seekers who surrounded it were likened to curiosity seekers in a morgue. It was reviled in scurrilous terms for its "immorality." Yet there is certainly nothing suggestive about *Olympia*. Quite the reverse. It is not exactly clinical in its objectivity, but it is not far from it. Salon, and public, ideas of morality in painting are enlighteningly demonstrated if *Olympia* is compared with *The Birth of Venus* (*Figure 7*) by the successful academician Alexandre Cabanel (1823–1889), which the emperor had purchased from the Salon of 1863. Its success brought Cabanel the ribbon of the Legion of Honor.

The Birth of Venus is so audacious a nude that the critics were forced into aesthetic gymnastics to defend it. They spoke of the wantonness of the Venus herself, but managed to find "purity" in the drawing to counteract it. Their safest ground was that this, after all, was a classical subject. That it was classical in name only made no difference. Even the most elementary comparison of the picture with

Figure 8

Botticelli's version of the same subject (Plates D 1 and D 2), or with any Venus of antiquity, even the most sensuous (Plate A 2), should show that Cabanel's goddess is no goddess but an expertly painted facsimile of a pretty model in a seductive pose. Not quite salacious in itself, the picture could be salaciously enjoyed by the salacious-minded under the protection of a pseudocultural veneer. Yet *Olympia* was "immoral" because it offered no opportunity for such subterfuge.

As a subject, *Olympia* is plainly and frankly and openly what it is, without moral comment or implication in any direction. The attacks on its "immorality" were stimulated in large part by a factor having nothing to do with the subject—the originality of Manet's technique, which demanded acceptance of a standard that violated academic formula, the formula so expertly applied by Cabanel. Among the minor

elements of this recipe for painting was the rule that the darks in a picture were painted first, then the half tones, lights, and finally high lights built up from them in an orderly fashion. Manet, however, applied his broad light areas first, sometimes over the whole area of the object, and into these lights he struck or brushed his shadows. That he did so is apparent to anyone who has practiced painting, just as it is apparent that he did so for a purpose. But to a school of painters who worked first by rule and only second if at all by reason, the heresy was shocking. It was also infuriating, since the effectiveness of Manet's way of painting was undeniable. *Olympia*'s ability to shock was an indirect tribute to the success of Manet's effort to create an image of immediate and convincing reality. We are in the very presence of the almost brashly self-confident little courtesan, but we are once removed from

Cabanel's studio Venus, in a way comparable to our removal from the performers on the stage of the Folies Bergère by the proscenium, the footlights, and all the prettifying trumpery of a theatrical spectacle.

Olympia's antecedents in the Renaissance are even more direct than those of *The Picnic*. Titian's *Venus of Urbino* (*Figure 8*) is the most obvious ancestor in the general disposition of the parts of the composition. Instead of two serving women in a recessed area, Manet has given us a single one in the foreground, a change consistent with the over-all flattening of form and what we might call the "suddenness" of effect. If we imagine a deep recess to the right in *Olympia* we must imagine also a secondary source of light and complications of perspective which, by asking the eye to assimilate images at different scales and different intensities, would reduce the impact of the foreground. In the Titian these complications enrich the picture, for it is one that may be explored and savored.

This may sound as if *Olympia*, on the other hand, is exhausted at a glance. But it, too, may be explored and savored in another way. We have already said that the genius of Manet is to crystallize a moment convincingly; as such a crystallization the image does not pall but continues to fascinate us; the moment is suspended in time. But beyond that, *Olympia* is an inexhaustible pleasure as art for art's sake. This concept, that a work of art may find its reason for being in itself rather than in what it "says" or is "about," was utterly foreign to the anecdotal idea that dominated Salon painting. In *Olympia* the abstract elements of form, color, arrangement, line, and, as well, the sheer manipulation of pigment are the primary interest of the painter, and they may be the primary interest of the observer, since they do not serve a moral, a religious, or a sensuous ideal as they do in other great paintings. In this way, *Olympia* is prophetic of those modern paintings in which such abstract elements are to exist entirely free of images.

Barbizon

In beginning with Courbet and his realistic revolt we passed by a quieter revolution that had already begun in the fields and along the riverbanks near Paris. Its participants were men slightly older than Courbet; among them we will see Théodore Rousseau (1812–1867) and Jean François Millet (1814–1875), whose birth dates can be compared with Courbet's (1819). Their realism, like Courbet's, was strongly flavored by romantic response to their subjects. These men were the Barbizon painters.

Barbizon is a small village thirty miles or so from Paris, where living was inexpensive and rural subjects were abundant. (Today the village is a rather self-consciously picturesque spot selling souvenirs of the artists who used to work there.) The Barbizon painters were not an organized school; only Rousseau and Millet spent a great deal of time there, but the name has attached itself to a group of artists who sometimes visited the village and shared an interest in painting nature in nature's presence. Although Courbet often did preliminary sketching in the countryside, the landscapes for his finished canvases were later fabricated indoors, as we can see in *The Painter's Studio*, where he works on one at an easel. The Barbizon painters were closer in their reference to nature; they completed more pictures on the spot (although they also worked in their studios). Above all, they were moved by nature's most humble and intimate aspects.

It may seem inconsistent to call this interest revolutionary when we have seen that Constable and other Englishmen had established a comparable tradition across the Channel. The point is that it was revolutionary in France where it affected the major development of the second half of the century, impressionism, while the English development remained relatively self-contained.

Just what was this "revolution"? Again it had to do with rejection of Salon standards, which attached importance only to studio-synthesized landscapes in the classical tradition. It was a rediscovery of nature, of nature not as a source for forms of trees, hills, streams, and skies that could be formalized into an ideal, but as a living world in which the cycle of night and day, of the seasons, of growth, decay, and rebirth, of sowing and reaping was intimately associated with the welfare and destiny of man. It was a world that did not demand grandiose manifestations to declaim its wonders but could reveal them in the most ordinary corner of a field.

When Turner painted a sunset he created a vision of cosmic fire consuming matter, turning great waters into pools of molten brass and streaking through the sky from horizon to firmament. But there is nothing visionary about a sunset by Rousseau (Plate 18). He paints the end of a day, an hour in a benign cycle, a special aspect of a countryside that remains ordinary, and loved. In his more detailed pictures Rousseau paints with such passionate absorption in the exact shape of a tree, the exact disposition of a leaf, the exact bend of blades of grass, that we see him as a pantheist for whom the world was a concentration of miracles. He is a realist in that he imitated nature closely; he is a romantic in that this imitation is based on his conviction that nature is so wonderful that merely to make images of it is a form of worship.

Rousseau's early career was a struggle. He

Figure 9

Figure 10

was refused from the Salon so many years in succession that he acquired the nickname "le grand refusé." But by the 1850s he and the other Barbizon painters had begun to come into their own. Their art had a natural appeal to a public that was developing a nostalgic love of the countryside, a nostalgia that increased as urbanization increasingly restricted their lives. And as far as the Academy was concerned, landscape was an art of secondary importance in which a few innovations were not too threatening. In addition, the Barbizon men had a modesty that contrasted with Courbet's truculence; and, finally, they were adopted by the young Georges Durand-Ruel, a dealer of genius, whose taste was to affect the course of art for the rest of the century. The jury of 1855 that rejected *The Painter's Studio* awarded Rousseau a Medal First Class, and in 1867, the year of his death, he received the Grand Medal of Honor. The intervening scandals of *The Picnic* and *Olympia* had made his work seem entirely conventional.

Millet, whose *The Sower* and *The Man with the Hoe* we have already discussed (Portfolio 11), is the most familiar of the Barbizon painters to tens of thousands of people who continue to love these pictures and the equally familiar *The Angelus* (*Figure 9*). Millet saw the peasant as a symbol of man's identification with the earth. He is one expression of the continuing "love of simple things" that we have discussed in connection with the Le Nains (Plate F 12) and Chardin (Plate G 5). Yet that unpleasant character, the Count of Nieuwerkerke, could say of pictures like *The Sower*, *The Angelus*, and *Woman with a Rake* (Plate I 9), "This is the painting of men who don't change their linen, who want to intrude themselves upon gentlemen; this art offends me and disgusts me." Today's critics would be more likely to find fault on the opposite score, that Millet has idealized his peasants to such an extent that their nobility is a bit oppressive, and that their earthiness has been lost in a general cleaning up.

Millet shared, somewhat precariously, the later popularity of the Barbizon painters. After his death prices for his work skyrocketed when Barbizon pictures were avidly collected, particularly in America. Not long ago, only thirty or forty years, his reputation still seemed firm;

Figure 11

but it has tobogganed along with others in the reaction against sentimental realism. But critics who reject *The Angelus* are discovering that a large group of less well-known works like *Woman with a Rake* and the unpretentious *Goose Girl* establish Millet as an artist who deserves more respect than it has been fashionable, lately, to give him.

The enduring and increasing reputation connected with Barbizon is that of Jean Baptiste Camille Corot (1796–1875). Corot's misty, gently poetic landscapes were tremendously popular. The emperor bought his *Souvenir de Marcoussis* from the banner Salon of 1855, not as official patronage but because he liked it. In that year, also, Corot won a Medal First Class. He knew and respected the Barbizon painters and worked occasionally in the vicinity. Some of his landscapes connect him with the Barbizon spirit, but he is beyond schools, a quiet individualist whose thoughtful and sensitive art draws upon the basic traditions of French painting without subjugation to any arbitrary standards.

In his cityscapes Corot revitalized Poussin's classical tradition. His views of Rome were painted as loving records of place (*Figure 10*), and they respect the actual disposition of buildings, trees, and hills. Yet they have the quiet and the completeness of Poussin's carefully synthesized compositions. Corot achieves the apparently impossible harmony between factual reality and classical synthesis by beginning with the disposition of architecture and topography, then adjusting the haphazard components into logical relationships by means of arbitrary tonalities. He may represent distant objects with greater clarity than the eye could see them. Or he may eliminate detail in nearby objects, detail which would concentrate interest on those areas sufficiently to overbalance the total scheme. He lightens a tone here, darkens a tone there, until in the end a picture of Rome as it existed when he saw it is as carefully adjusted as the nonexistent city that Poussin invented in *The Funeral of Phocion* (Portfolio 7, Plate 76).

The most prized Corots today are those least known in his lifetime, the figure studies painted for his own enjoyment and seldom exhibited. Ordinarily these are of young women, pensive, even faintly melancholy, some-

Figure 12

times costumed as "gypsies" or other nominally romantic figures, perhaps against a suggestion of landscape, sometimes seated in a quiet room, a corner of Corot's studio, holding a book or a musical instrument. *The Letter* (Plate I 10) is one of these; in its apparently casual pose, in its unpretentious scale, with its air of gentleness and naturalness, its lack of all pretension, it is at first acquaintance an utterly charming bit of painting, a little picture of tremendous attraction. But it is more than this. Upon longer acquaintance its quietness deepens, its harmonies reveal new subtleties, its forms take on more conclusive balance, and its reverie is enriched by truly classic serenity.

Daumier

While the Barbizon painters were setting up their easels in the fields, while Courbet was propounding realism as a theory, while Manet was painting *The Picnic* and *Olympia*, a great realist known to all these men was presenting his work in a stream of thousands of examples to a delighted public. Yet he was quite apart from the furor of art circles. He was Honoré Daumier (1808–1879), who produced more than five thousand lithographs in the form of cartoons for Paris journals, and almost in secret painted some of the masterpieces of nineteenth-century realism.

Daumier's cartoons range from hilarious farce to powerful social and political comment. But whether he shows us a bourgeois family suffering comical indignities at the zoo (*Figure 11*) or the victims of war rising in accusation against the demagogues who have cost them their lives (*Figure 12*), he is one of the master draughtsmen of any time. He was self-trained. Insofar as he had masters, they were Rembrandt and Michelangelo by example. But his eye was his true teacher. As he observed the Parisian crowd going about their business he studied the way they moved, the set of the features in their heads, the structure of bone protruding through sagging muscles

Figure 13

or the bulk of a fat belly propelled along the street by a pair of skinny legs.

Where Courbet adopted a half-understood political philosophy as a form of self-dramatization, Daumier courageously and unyieldingly propagandized for republican ideals during a succession of regimes that violated them. He was imprisoned for six months, when he was twenty-four, for a cartoon called *Gargantua* showing Louis Philippe swallowing bags of gold extracted from the people. When he attacked corruption, sham, or injustice, Daumier was merciless, but his comments on the lesser foibles of his fellow man are as benign as they are clear-sighted. He satirized the conflict between the realists and the academic idealists in a good-natured take-off (*Figure 13*) on the two warriors who face one another in David's *The Sabines* (Portfolio H, *Figure 3*). The Sabine Tatius, on the left, a caricature of the realists' self-conscious earthiness, becomes a rough little fellow who would certainly "offend and disgust" the Count of Nieuwerkerke, while David's slickly beautiful Romulus is de-idealized into a skinny pedant whose shrunken hams and absurd face are inadequate accessories to his pretensions. The reason this figure is so funny is that it is so logical. Its comical exaggerations are drawn with faultless knowledge of the construction of the human body and an unerring selection of the most telling points for the desired effect. Daumier's

Figure 14

Romulus, a caricature, is at least as brilliant as David's Romulus, an idealization.

Daumier gave as much time to painting as he could spare from his job, but he made little effort to market these. His first collective exhibition was in 1878. By that time the realist revolt had run its course. Courbet had died the year before; Corot, Rousseau, and Millet were also dead; the impressionists were the new scandal. Thus the first exhibition of one of the earliest realists of the century came when the movement had become history. Daumier himself died the following year, in poverty and nearly blind. He had been saved from complete pennilessness by Corot, who had given him a small house in the country some years before, and by a small pension from the Third Republic. Nevertheless he was buried in a pauper's grave. A syndicate bought his hundreds of paintings, for a pittance, from his widow.

Later when they were put on the market, augmented by numerous forgeries that are still causing confusion, they brought a fortune.

Daumier's paintings reveal his love and respect for the honest, inconspicuous, hard-pressed human being who lives out his obscure middle-class life in the anonymity of the city crowd. But he also did many pictures of peasants. His *Third-Class Carriage* (*Figure 14*) could have shown Millet that the nobility of simple people can be revealed in terms less idealized than those of *The Angelus*, or even of the *Woman with a Rake*, and that man's union with the basic forces of life may be as apparent in a railway car as it is in the fields.

Homer and Eakins

In America during these years, painting was thought of as a polite adjunct to gracious living

24

for those who could afford to patronize the arts or as a sentimental moral demonstration (*Breaking Home Ties*) by people who were "interested in art." Salon painting was imported as gilt-edged merchandise and brought the highest prices in culturally ambitious circles. By preference American artists studied in Europe and did their best to meet Salon standards after they came home. By denying their birthright most of them ended up neither one thing nor another, with the result that the history of American painting as we now see it is the history of a few men who were nonconformists in ways that made their expression more purely American—a paradox. There was virtually no self-conscious Americanism among artists of the kind that became a cult for a while in the twentieth century.

The two most genuinely American painters of the latter half of the nineteenth century were Winslow Homer (1836–1910), who was four years younger than Manet, and Thomas Eakins (1844–1916), who was an even closer contemporary of the impressionists but had no affiliations with them, even at long distance. In searching for a native tradition, American critics have found one in men whose forthright realism reflects the vigor, the practicality, the natural honesty, and the democratic unpretentiousness that we like to think of as national characteristics. Certainly Homer and Eakins both demonstrate these qualities in their cen-

Figure 15

25

tury as Peale and Copley did in the eighteenth.

Homer's *Gloucester Farm* (Plate I 11) is one of his group of early pictures of New England subjects, a beautiful little painting whose virtues are so apparent, so open, so independent of theorizing or unusual problem-solving that they hardly need pointing out. The fresh light of early morning, the attractive sturdiness of the young people, the succinct definition of locale by a barn and some half-seen animals, the bit of rustic narrative, all are the elements of genre painting at a superior level. Homer raises the picture even beyond that level by the economy and solidity of his forms and their arrangement. Thus he invests an inconsequential scene with the importance and dignity that Millet strove for more ambitiously. By comparison, Millet's point seems forced. Homer does not say to us, self-consciously, that he is painting with a program in mind, and his picture is doubly effective for this reticence.

In a later group of subjects Homer comes closer to this kind of self-consciousness. These are his scenes from the life of sailors and fishermen on the Grand Banks with their harsh rock coasts and heavy seas, painted after 1885 when he settled at Prout's Neck, Maine. The success of these pictures, as expressive ones, has been exaggerated by our admiration for Homer's exploration of uniquely American subjects. Yet *Eight Bells* (*Figure 15*), as one of the most admired, is certainly no more "American" than *Gloucester Farm*. Perhaps it is less so, for being more particularized.

Gloucester Farm, in spite of its early date, has affinities with impressionism, and in a long life Homer was to anticipate or parallel several impressionist innovations. After 1884 he began the trips to the West Indies that brought him into a new world of sparkling light and bright color. His water-color technique was especially affected, and in such examples as *Sloop, Bermuda* (Portfolio 10, Plate 111) he is an expert impressionist by fairly strict definition.

Homer won through to popularity and recognition in spite of the fact that the vigor and directness of his work went against the standards of what was considered really fine art. But "fine" art continued to bring the high prices, and he was never very successful financially. The fact that he was an innovator was hardly noticed in a country where the public was barely conscious of the battle of styles on the other side of the Atlantic.

Homer had his own opinion of "fine" art, and he could be a thorny opponent in an argument. But he was more interested in painting as he pleased than in setting up a camp and defending it. For that matter, American interest in painting was not of the kind to support a battle of styles. Thomas Eakins, a Philadelphian eight years younger than Homer, was more forceful in his formulation and defense of standards running counter to conventional ones, and he suffered more as a result in commissions lost, clients dissatisfied, and finally with authorities offended, so that he lost his position as a teacher at the Pennsylvania Academy of Fine Arts. But, again because painting was not a subject of much

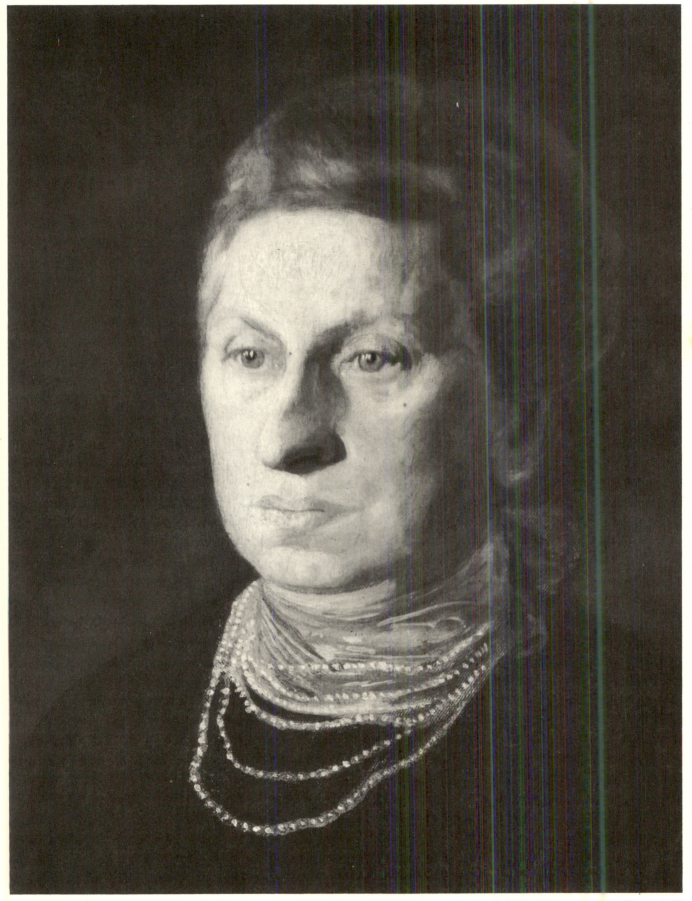

Figure 17

27

general concern, Eakins met his defeats as well as his successes in obscurity. Not that he was unknown: when John Singer Sargent, the outstanding portraitist of the day, visited Philadelphia and was asked whom he would like to meet, he asked for Eakins. But his fashionable hostess had never heard of this painter who had been born and raised and was still working in the city.

Eakins's passion was anatomy. He combined his early study (largely drawing from casts) at the Pennsylvania Academy with courses in dissection at Jefferson Medical College. The human body fascinated him, not as an ideal form, not as a symbol, but as an organism so constructed that it was capable of movement. To learn to draw it he went to Paris in 1866 to study under—of all people—Gérôme, at the École des Beaux Arts, the Academy-sponsored school.

He stayed four years, years during which *Olympia* was still the storm center of art. Yet from all evidence he was not interested in Manet or in anything but drawing from the model in the usual way. This "usual way" had its importance for Eakins, although by the end of his stay in Paris he recognized its limitations. In spite of all that was wrong with the academic approach creatively, academic training in drawing was sound and thorough. The training became meaningless only when it was used to serve sterile formulas for picturemaking, and for Eakins it was the acquisition of a means to an important end, the representation of the world, especially the people in the world, in realistic images that would carry with them his own responses to life.

Eakins's portrait of Mrs. William D. Frishmuth (*Figure 16*, detail, *Figure 17*) may show us why he was indifferent to Manet's experiments. We have said that *Olympia*, in its objectivity, is noninterpretative to the point where it becomes a work of art for art's sake; that the technique, exploring the nature of vision, is at once end and means. But for Eakins technique was purely an instrument. His brush

was to him as a painter very much what his scalpel had been when he dissected cadavers to satisfy at first hand his curiosity about the structure of bones and muscles. With his brush as an instrument he explores the nature of Mrs. Frishmuth, this calm, strong woman with the unlovely face. Through recreating this face in paint, as his subject sat before him, he reveals and immortalizes a personality. We may be certain that as a likeness the portrait is accurate. We cannot know exactly what subtle variations and accents account for the revelation of character—perhaps the brightening of an eye, the deepening of a shadow, the emphasizing of the peak of an eyebrow. But these subtleties, whatever they are, account for the difference between a portrait by Eakins and the kind of accurate but meaningless likenesses produced by hundreds of his contemporaries, and of ours. The genius of Eakins is that he perceives, and then reveals, the psychological entity of an individual, without apparent recourse to any but the most objective means.

Eakins supported himself by portraits and teaching, but like his impressionist contemporaries in France he also turned to the life of city folk as the natural subject for a painter in his time. Granted his interest in anatomy, this field led him to fighters in the prize ring and to rowers in their shells on the Schuylkill. And while Renoir and Monet were painting Parisians relaxing along the Seine, Eakins painted Philadelphians sailing on the Delaware or strolling its banks on a Sunday. The Frenchmen were developing new ways of representing the shimmer of light, were experimenting with color and composition. Eakins, essentially a traditionalist in the most honorable sense of the word, painted pictures like *Mending the Net* (Plate I 12) in a solidly traditional way. It is a picture which the impressionists, to whom Eakins was not even a familiar name, would have admired, with its grouping of figures along the horizon, so carefully studied yet so convincing in its effect of casualness.

Figure 18

As a group the five men and two little girls at left center (*Figure 18*) in themselves compose a frieze of rhythmic unity and variety that should be impossible, or at least disharmonious, when its units are studied in their commonplaceness and their naturalness. The men go about their task unconscious of our presence, and the little girls stand just as children do when they watch adults at work (and more naturally, by the way, than the little boy who watches Courbet in *The Painter's Studio*). Yet there is not a line, an attitude, a relationship, that we could change without disrupting the balanced harmony. That the picture is not quite finished may seem to contradict such a statement. The lines of the net, for instance, which are only suggested, would eventually have been stronger. One leg of the kneeling man is only sketched in from the knee down. But surely we can believe that each change or addition would have been accompanied by compensating ones. Eakins was one of those painters (like Cézanne) who built a picture so methodically and at once so sensitively that in all stages of its growth it seemed to have attained the certainty of its conclusion. The sobriety, the dignity, and the warm life of *Mending the Net* must have been present from the beginning, and in the hands of Eakins these qualities were never lost.

When Eakins died in 1916 not only had impressionism become history in Europe but cubism and fauvism had been born and had been introduced in America with the 1913 Armory Show. A Russian named Kandinsky had produced the first entirely abstract painting. Our concluding discussions will follow impressionism into the art of Cézanne and other painters who are the direct sources of contemporary art, and we will examine some of the multiple transformations of the art of painting in our century.

Color Plates

Figures in the Text